Mortified

Amy Rutherford

T0386269

PLAYWRIGHTS CANADA PRESS

TORONTO

Mortified © Copyright 2022 by Amy Rutherford

LIBRARY AND ARCHIVES CANADA CATALOGUING IN PUBLICATION
Title: Mortified / Amy Rutherford.
Names: Rutherford, Amy (Actor), author.
Description: A play.
Identifiers: Canadiana (print) 20210305991 | Canadiana (ebook) 2021030605X
  | ISBN 9780369102935 (softcover) | ISBN 9780369102942 (PDF)
  | ISBN 9780369102959 (HTML)
Classification: LCC PS8635.U8845 M67 2021 | DDC C812/.6—dc23

Playwrights Canada Press operates on land which is the ancestral home of the Anishinaabe Nations (Ojibwe / Chippewa, Odawa, Potawatomi, Algonquin, Saulteaux, Nipissing, and Mississauga), the Wendat, and the members of the Haudenosaunee Confederacy (Mohawk, Oneida, Onondaga, Cayuga, Seneca, and Tuscarora), as well as Metis and Inuit peoples. It always was and always will be Indigenous land.

We acknowledge the financial support of the Canada Council for the Arts, the Ontario Arts Council (OAC), Ontario Creates, and the Government of Canada for our publishing activities.

Canada Council   Conseil des arts
for the Arts   du Canada

ONTARIO ARTS COUNCIL
CONSEIL DES ARTS DE L'ONTARIO
an Ontario government agency
un organisme du gouvernement de l'Ontario

Canada   ONTARIO | ONTARIO
CREATES | CRÉATIF

For the teachers at RPA's First Place Program in Ottawa.
And for my table tennis coach, Mariann Domonkos.

Mortified was first produced by Studio 58 in association with Touchstone Theatre, Vancouver, in November 2018 with the following cast and artistic team:

Girl: Emily Jane King
Woman: Lindsey Angell
Coach Cindy: Jessie Liang
Ty: Ian Butcher
Young Ty: Isaac Mazur
Synchronized Swimmers: Julia Muncs, Paige Fraser, Hannah Pearson, Margaret Onedo, Lauren Preissl, Mariana Munoz, Katie Voravong
Ensemble: Daniel Bristol, Nicholas Elia, Moe Golkar, Jimmy JinPyo Hong, Isaac Li, Taylor Long, Nolan McConnell-Fidyk, Jarred Stephen Meek, Matisse Quaglia, Solomon Rise, Joe Rose, Ella Storey, Daniel Swain, David Underhill, Kelsey Kanatan Wavey

Director: Anita Rochon
Dramaturge: Jonathon Young
Set Design: Pam Johnson
Costume Design: Carman Alatorre
Lighting Design: Brad Trenaman
Sound Design: Malcolm Dow
Projection Design: Jordan Lloyd Watkins
Choreographer: Amber Funk Barton

"But, if you take my voice, what will be left to me?"

"Your lovely form," said the witch. "Your gliding movements, and your eloquent eyes. With these you can easily enchant a human heart. Have you lost your courage? Stick out your little tongue and I shall cut it off."
—Hans Christian Andersen, "The Little Mermaid"

Mine has been a life of much shame. I can't even guess myself what it must be to have a life of a human being.
—Osamu Dazai, *No Longer Human*

Cast

WOMAN: a woman in her forties

GIRL: the teenage version version of the Woman

TY: both a man in his fifties and a twenty-one-year-old wannabe pimp

COACH CINDY: an ancient and ageless synchronized swimming coach with magical powers

SYNCHRONIZED SWIMMER 1

SYNCHRONIZED SWIMMER 2

SYNCHRONIZED SWIMMER 3

SYNCHRONIZED SWIMMER 4

SYNCHRONIZED SWIMMER 5

The following roles are played by the five synchronized swimmers and could be divided like this:

SYNCHRONIZED SWIMMER 1
BROTHER: a university student majoring in women's studies
SANDY: a thirteen-year-old who prefers horses to people
SHANNON'S DAD: a cheery gentleman in his fifties
BEN: a thirteen-year-old wannabe bad boy

SYNCHRONIZED SWIMMER 2
BOY: a sensitive twelve-year-old boy
DAD: a hopeful and clueless father
SHANNON: a testy thirteen-year-old with a walker

SYNCHRONIZED SWIMMER 3
MOM: a worried and protective mother
ANDY: a thirteen-year-old boy who wants to be a werewolf
DONNY: a thirteen-year-old boy with a huge bulge in his pants
ZACH: a creepy guy in his twenties wearing a gold chain

SYNCHRONIZED SWIMMER 4
SISTER: a sixteen-year-old full of rage
JANINE: a thirteen-year-old girl who loves doodling and egg salad
BELINDA: a thirteen-year-old New Kids on the Block fan

SYNCHRONIZED SWIMMER 5
ALISHA: a worldly and charismatic fourteen-year-old

Production Notes

Cast size is flexible. Though *Mortified* was initially conceived as a play for nine performers (eight female, one male), its premiere production in Vancouver featured a mixed-gender cast of twenty-seven. With such a large cast, each performer was able to inhabit a single character, with the synchronized swimming team becoming a distinct unit within the larger group. Two actors played Ty, one in the present and one in the past. The distribution of lines and roles among the synchronized swimmers is flexible when it improves the clarity and efficiency of storytelling. If possible, Coach Cindy's narration should be amplified and can be performed live or as a voice-over when necessary.

Notes On Dialogue

Keeping up the pace is important. Unless a transition is indicated, each scene should flow into the next. Italicized text indicates stage directions or special emphasis.

A forward slash (/) in the middle of a sentence indicates the start of an overlap by the next character's line.

An em dash (—) at the end of a line indicates the character is cut off.

An ellipsis (...) indicates a trailing off or searching.

Act 1

Scene 1

A GIRL is alone in what appears to be the bottom of a decrepit old pool. COACH CINDY watches her from above, on a diving board.

COACH CINDY: A girl in the body of a woman. Stuck between this world and another. Longing to be human again.

A WOMAN appears.

GIRL: Do you have smokes?

WOMAN: No.

GIRL: Yeah you do. Gimme one.

WOMAN: No.

GIRL: Why not?

WOMAN: I quit.

GIRL: Liar.

> *Beat.*

So why are you here? You obviously have something you want to say.

WOMAN: I don't.

GIRL: Then what do you want?

WOMAN: *Hush!*

GIRL: You're creeping me out.

WOMAN: I need to think.

GIRL: Thinking's boring. Why can't we conversate?

WOMAN: That's not a word.

GIRL: Yeah it is.

WOMAN: "*Conversate*"?

Beat.

GIRL: Fine. Don't mind me. I'll just be over here . . . *rotting.*

WOMAN: I ran into your boyfriend today.

GIRL: Ty!? You ran into Ty? Where?

WOMAN: In the food court. At the mall. Paul went to get us smoothies and I turned around and . . . there he was.

GIRL: Did he see you?

WOMAN: Yeah. I looked away but it was too late. He came over and, and he—*hugged* me.

GIRL: Uh huh. And?

WOMAN: *I hugged him back.*

GIRL: What did he smell like?

WOMAN: The same.

GIRL: Like hair wax?

WOMAN: I guess.

GIRL: And pot?

WOMAN: Probably.

GIRL: And the inside of a cardboard box?

WOMAN: Yeah.

GIRL: It's his hair. He never washes it.

WOMAN: His hair's all gone.

GIRL: Gone?

WOMAN: He's bald.

GIRL: Oh. Did you guys talk about me?

WOMAN: No.

GIRL: Why not?

WOMAN: I'm not opening that up again. I'm not going to talk to *Ty* about *you*.

The GIRL grabs at the WOMAN.

Hey! Get off of me—what are you doing?

GIRL: Stop ignoring me.

The GIRL grabs at the WOMAN again.

WOMAN: Stop! Get your hand out of my—

GIRL: Don't! You're pulling my hair. Ow, ow, / ow, ow!

WOMAN: Don't be so dramatic.

GIRL: You suck.

WOMAN: You suck.

GIRL: You suck.

WOMAN: Stop behaving like a—

GIRL: I know you are but what am I?

WOMAN: Oh, okay, I get it. This is the part / where you—

GIRL: I know you are but / what am I?

WOMAN: Now you're just being—

GIRL: I know you are but what / am I?

WOMAN: Aaaargh!

The WOMAN exits, leaving the GIRL behind.

COACH CINDY: A girl. In the body of a woman. Longing to be human again.

Transition. The GIRL looks up at a shadow passing overhead.

Scene 2

A BOY enters. It is nighttime. Moonlight reflects off the water. We can hear the sound of the waves lapping against the shore.

BOY: You won't be coming back?

GIRL: No.

BOY: Never?

COACH CINDY: Her family moves cities when the Girl is thirteen.

GIRL: I don't know. It's really far.

BOY: How are you getting there?

GIRL: We're driving.

BOY: In the Oldsma?

GIRL: Yeah. Don't be sad.

BOY: I'm not.

    Beat.

Don't you have to speak French in Ottawa?

GIRL: I hope not. The only words I know are "bleu" and "je m'appelle."

BOY: What about synchro?

GIRL: My mom says they have the best team in the country.

BOY: But it's better here.

GIRL: How do you know?

BOY: Do you want to be near the ocean or a slimy canal? You should move in with us. I'll ask my parents.

GIRL: My mom wouldn't let me.

Beat. The BOY has an idea

BOY: I know! Get them to take you to the beach. One more time before you go. And then swim out, like, really far. I can meet you on a raft.

GIRL: Okay. Do you have a raft?

BOY: No, but I'll build one.

GIRL: How?

BOY: Out of sticks and branches. The main challenge is that you'll have to stay under water, so as not to be seen by the coast guard. You got a snorkel?

GIRL: No. But I can hold my breath.

BOY: How long?

GIRL: Three minutes?

BOY: That's not enough!

He starts to cry.

GIRL: It's okay . . .

BOY: It's a stupid plan. It won't work!

GIRL: I'm sorry.

> *The GIRL hugs him, and he calms down. There is a moment of awkward intimacy.*

BOY: Dinkus?

GIRL: Yeah?

> *A Big Turk is thrown on stage. The BOY catches it.*

BOY: I bought you a Big Turk.

GIRL: Thanks.

BOY: Bye, dork.

GIRL: Bye, loser.

BOY: Send me a postcard of the Parliament Buildings.

COACH CINDY: The Girl waves out the back window of her family's Oldsma as the Boy grows smaller and smaller in the distance. His bottom lip quivering, he chokes back tears. She can feel the Big Turk in her hand, melting in its wrapper, as the car takes a sharp turn east.

> *The BOY exits.*

Scene 3

The GIRL is in a car with her family. Her BROTHER and SISTER sit on either side of her. Her MOM sits up front with her DAD, who is whistling.

SISTER: *(thrashing as if possessed)* Aaarrrghhh!

GIRL: Mom! She's opening her door! What do I do?

MOM: Honey, don't do that. Do we need to pull over?

DAD: How about a song? "The Wheels on the Bus," anyone? / "The wheels on the bus go round and round, / round and round, round and round. The wheels on the bus go round and round, all through the town."

SISTER: No, Dad! Stooooop . . . That's annoying! Stop!!!!

MOM: Maybe you should stop.

SISTER: It's so hot!!

MOM: Then open a window, honey!

SISTER: It doesn't help!! Dad. Stop. *Singing*!

DAD: "The wipers on the bus go swish swish swish, / swish swish swish, swish swish swish. The wipers on bus go swish swish swish, all through the town."

GIRL: You can come to my side, there's less sun . . .

The GIRL's SISTER climbs over her BROTHER.

SISTER: Ah!!!!

BROTHER: Hey! Settle down!

SISTER: I hate you!

BROTHER: How much farther is it!?

SISTER: Get me out of this hellhole!

DAD: Only thirty-eight hours to go!

SISTER: I. NEED / . . .

GIRL: She needs air—

MOM: She needs?

GIRL, SISTER, & BROTHER: Air!!!

MOM: Husky station!!!

The family pulls over and the GIRL and her SISTER get out of the car.

SISTER: Aaaaah . . .

MOM: *(calling out)* In and out, girls. Mind your pees and poos. And *be careful.*

Scene 4

The GIRL and her SISTER split away from their parents.

GIRL: Are you okay?

SISTER: No. I got drunk last night and woke up topless in the mouth of the Concrete Monster.

GIRL: In the playground at the school?

SISTER: No, stupid. In a real monster. What do you think?

GIRL: How did you get home?

SISTER: I ran as fast as I could with my eyes closed so I wouldn't have to see anyone looking at me. I'm glad we're moving. I never want to see those losers again.

Her SISTER exits.

Scene 5

The WOMAN enters with her hand wrapped in a bloody dishtowel.

WOMAN: Out of the way, out of the way, out of the way—

GIRL: What is it now?

WOMAN: I fuh! I fuh! I fuh!

GIRL: You—

WOMAN: I fucking punched a knife!

GIRL: You punched a . . .

WOMAN: We were making dinner, Paul and I, stuffing squids—

GIRL: Gross.

WOMAN: I'm chopping at the counter, and Paul asks me, "Who was that guy?" and I say, "Who was that guy?" and he says, "Yeah, who was that guy? That weird guy at the mall," and I don't know what to say, so I fucking punched a knife!

GIRL: Why?

WOMAN: Why?

GIRL: Why didn't you just tell him?

The WOMAN grabs the GIRL.

WOMAN: "Paul, listen!"

GIRL: Am I . . . ?

WOMAN: "Paul."

GIRL: I'm Paul?

WOMAN: Just listen! "Paul."

GIRL: Yes?

WOMAN: "I need to tell you something. You may *think* that I'm lying, but I'm not—"

GIRL: Okay . . .

WOMAN: I'm telling you—

GIRL: "It's okay, honey."

WOMAN: —the *truth*. Even if right now in this moment it feels like I'm *not* being truthful, because I'm telling you that I *will* be truthful, I *am* being truthful. And I will be. Truthful."

GIRL: 'Kay.

WOMAN: Do I seem like I'm lying?

GIRL: Yes.

WOMAN: Are my eyes looking up to the right? Like this?

GIRL: Now they are.

WOMAN: Liars do that. They smirk and their eyes look up to the right, like this.

The WOMAN darts her eyes up to the right repeatedly.

GIRL: What's the big deal? He loves you, doesn't he?

WOMAN: Who?

GIRL: Paul!

WOMAN: How am I supposed to know?

GIRL: Because you love him, right?

WOMAN: Mm hm.

GIRL: Right?

WOMAN: Yes.

Beat.

Yes.

Beat.

I feel like I'm lying again. Why!? Why do I always feel like I'm lying?
I *do* love him. And he loves me. He told me. He *tells* me. We *love* each
other.

GIRL: So stop punching knives and just tell him what's wrong.

WOMAN: I can't.

GIRL: You can't?

WOMAN: I'm not that sort of person.

GIRL: What sort of person—

WOMAN: The sort of person who—I can't just, it's not— I can't just—

GIRL: Just—?

WOMAN: —*"fall into someone!"*

Beat.

GIRL: But he's out there stuffing squids.

WOMAN: Right. And I'm hiding in here like some diseased sea animal,
wanting to disappear, resenting him for not knowing something I've
told him nothing about.

GIRL: Yeah, no one wants to be around that.

WOMAN: Exactly. It's best not to say anything.

GIRL: I didn't say that!

The WOMAN exits.

Wait! Come back! Stay with me!

Scene 6

The GIRL's MOM and DAD enter.

DAD: You can't fight it, kiddo! Today's the day!

MOM: Brand new outfit!

DAD: Chop, chop! Tick tick! Gotta go!

MOM: Here, honey, quick!

MOM fusses with the GIRL's clothes.

GIRL: What are you—

MOM steps back.

MOM: Perfect! You look great. Doesn't she, honey? With her jelly shoes and her little heart-shaped earrings?

GIRL: *(privately to her DAD)* I don't want to go in.

DAD: Sweetheart, you're a big girl now. See this as an opportunity to make new friends. A whole new school.

COACH CINDY: She opens the front doors and steps into a sea of stinking boys and girls.

MOM and DAD wave to the GIRL as the SYNCHRONIZED SWIMMERS enter.

DAD: Take your pick!

MOM and DAD exit.

Scene 7

JANINE: I'm Janine. I doodle incessantly while shoving egg salad into my mouth with my fingers.

SANDY: I'm Sandy. I have a mane of long, blond hair and prefer horses to people.

BELINDA: I'm Belinda. I wear purple jewellery. I carry a lot of candy in my New Kids on the Block purse, and I don't notice you.

ANDY: I'm Andy, and I'm a werewolf.

SHANNON enters.

SHANNON: I'm Shannon. I'm about three feet tall and I smell like a hospital room. I use a walker even though I'm not old. I'm the only one who shows any real interest in you, even if it is hostile, even if it is just a steady glare from beneath a prominent unibrow.

GIRL: Hi, Shannon.

SHANNON: *(feigning fright)* Ah!

GIRL: Sorry, did I scare you?

SHANNON: You're very pale.

GIRL: I am?

SHANNON: Like a ghost.

GIRL: Oh.

SHANNON: Or a ghoul.

GIRL: Isn't that the same thing?

SHANNON: No, a ghost is just a displaced spirit, a ghoul eats the stolen corpses of children. You're pale like a ghost and dark under your eyes like a ghoul.

GIRL: Oh.

SHANNON: You're skinny like a scarecrow, and your arms are grotesquely muscular like a man's.

> *The GIRL's classmates laugh and exit, leaving her alone with SHANNON.*

GIRL: We need to split off into groups for our next project. Would you like to pair up?

SHANNON: If I have to . . .

> *SHANNON starts to leave. She's moving very slowly . . .*

Are you coming?

> *The GIRL follows.*

GIRL: Do you need my—

SHANNON: Don't! I can do it myself!

GIRL: Sorry.

SHANNON: Don't be sorry, just don't be pushy!

COACH CINDY: Shannon leads the Girl to her home. The Girl shortens her step, so as not to get ahead.

Scene 8

SHANNON'S DAD enters.

SHANNON'S DAD: Oh, hello there! Welcome! You must be Shannon's friend. I've heard so much about—

SHANNON: *Dad.*

SHANNON'S DAD: I'll go fix you girls a snack.

SHANNON'S DAD exits.

GIRL: Your room's so clean.

SHANNON: I don't clean it. My dad does.

SHANNON'S DAD re-enters with two plates of sandwiches.

SHANNON'S DAD: Here we are! I'm a whiz with the Whiz!

SHANNON refuses to look at her DAD. SHANNON'S DAD hands the GIRL a plate.

I call them Whiz Sandwiches.

SHANNON: Cheez Whiz and hot dog buns.

SHANNON'S DAD: Shannon's favourite.

SHANNON: *You can go now.*

COACH CINDY: Shannon glares at the Girl, wheezing, then takes a bite of her Whiz Sandwich. The Girl is distracted by the fluorescent yellow snot encrusted around the tubes in her nose and the dangling bag on the side of her body that looks to be filling with . . .

The GIRL takes a bite of the sandwich and gags.

SHANNON: You don't have to eat it.

GIRL: What?

SHANNON: If my dad's cooking's grossing you out.

GIRL: Kinda.

SHANNON: Just put them on the window ledge and the birds will take it.

GIRL: Really?

SHANNON: *(nodding)* Mm hm.

GIRL: Okay . . . I'll put them on the window ledge.

The GIRL places her plate on the window ledge and the lights in the room suddenly dim.

SHANNON: *(slowly moving in on the GIRL)* They can see more than we do. Birds. They can see the earth's magnetic field. They can see behind themselves. When attacked, they go directly for the eyes of their adversary. They attack before being attacked.

Birds caw and shriek outside the window.

GIRL: Are you making this up?

SHANNON: No.

She breaks away from the GIRL. *The lights return to normal as* SHANNON'S DAD *re-enters.*

SHANNON'S DAD: How were the Whiz Sandwiches?

GIRL: Good!

SHANNON: *(turning on the* GIRL*)* Liar. She didn't eat hers!

SHANNON'S DAD: *(also turning)* You didn't—

GIRL: Yeah, I did.

SHANNON: She put them on the window ledge!

GIRL: No, I didn't—

SHANNON'S DAD: *(wounded)* You could have just told me that you didn't like them.

GIRL: I didn't mean to . . . I'm sorry.

SHANNON: You're not sorry. You thought they were gross and disgusting. You think I'm gross and disgusting. You didn't actually want to be my friend. You just didn't have a partner for the science project and you felt sorry for me. On the surface you're "nice," but deep down you don't give a shit.

GIRL: You *told* me to put them on the ledge!

SHANNON: She didn't pass the Cheez Whiz Test.

GIRL: I want to take it again!

SHANNON: She's a liar. You're a liar!

COACH CINDY: When she returns home, the Girl draws the blue curtains shut, to catch the evening sun, and imagines that she is submerged in an underwater kingdom.

Transition.

Scene 9

Swim practice with COACH CINDY. *The* SYNCHRONIZED SWIMMERS *do synchronized drills as they speak their lines.*

COACH CINDY: It's called *synchronized* swimming. If you're doing it on your own, you're not doing it. How do you know you're doing it?

SYNCHRONIZED SWIMMERS: It hurts!

COACH CINDY: This is not a solo!

SYNCHRONIZED SWIMMERS: This is not a solo!

COACH CINDY: If you're pushing someone up for a boost and you can't feel the crushing weight of your teammates—

SYNCHRONIZED SWIMMER 1: *(aside to the* GIRL*)* Coach Cindy never smiles.

COACH CINDY: —their toenails digging into your shoulders—

SYNCHRONIZED SWIMMER 2: She actually can't smile.

COACH CINDY: —as your legs move as fast as egg beaters beneath you—

SYNCHRONIZED SWIMMER 3: She's incapable of smiling.

COACH CINDY: —it's not happening!

SYNCHRONIZED SWIMMER 4: So don't go looking for it.

SYNCHRONIZED SWIMMER 2: That's not her real face.

GIRL: It isn't?

SYNCHRONIZED SWIMMER 3: She smashed her real face into the end of the pool and it had to be reconstructed.

COACH CINDY: If you don't feel an elbow in the side of your gut, a heel in the back of your head— If you don't feel like you're doing a hundred-metre sprint, underwater, with your nose plugged, half-blind, holding your breath—like you're being *waterboarded*, like you're going to *die*, you're not doing it!!! Trust me. I know. I survived Sarajevo.

SYNCHRONIZED SWIMMER 4: *(to the GIRL)* The Olympics.

COACH CINDY turns violently to SYNCHRONIZED SWIMMER 4.

COACH CINDY: What's that?

SYNCHRONIZED SWIMMER 5: . . . The '84 Olympics in Sarajevo?

COACH CINDY: *(suspiciously)* Uh huh. And I have a medal to prove it.

SYNCHRONIZED SWIMMER 4: Coach Cindy can see right through to your heart's desire.

SYNCHRONIZED SWIMMER 1: Like a witch.

SYNCHRONIZED SWIMMER 2: Seriously.

GIRL: A witch?

SYNCHRONIZED SWIMMER 3: If a woman can win a bronze medal at the Olympics after smashing her face in—

SYNCHRONIZED SWIMMER 2: If she can cure two girls of bulimia and make them national champions—

SYNCHRONIZED SWIMMER 4: Is it so hard to believe that she has magical, psychic powers too?

COACH CINDY: I've seen girls rise to the top and I've seen them sink to the bottom. Listen to me and you'll double your lung capacity and be national champions. Show up on time!

SYNCHRONIZED SWIMMERS: Show up on time!

COACH CINDY: Sequin your *own* suits, practise land drills at home!

SYNCHRONIZED SWIMMERS: Land drills at home!

COACH CINDY: Go to bed early.

SYNCHRONIZED SWIMMER 1: Sleep eight hours a night!

COACH CINDY: Eat well!

SYNCHRONIZED SWIMMERS 1 & 2: Protein!

SYNCHRONIZED SWIMMERS 3 & 4: Powder!

COACH CINDY: We don't want you skinny. We don't want you fat. We don't want you short. We don't want you tall. We want you just . . . right. Shaved—

SYNCHRONIZED SWIMMERS: Taut—

COACH CINDY: Toned! *Toned!*

SYNCHRONIZED SWIMMERS: Shaved!

COACH CINDY: Taut!

SYNCHRONIZED SWIMMERS: Synchronized . . .

SYNCHRONIZED SWIMMERS 1, 2, 3, and 4 exit.

Scene 10

SYNCHRONIZED SWIMMER 5 remains as ALISHA.

ALISHA: I like your earrings.

GIRL: *(flattered)* Thanks . . .

(seeing ALISHA's pants) I like your . . .

ALISHA: They're stirrups.

GIRL: What?

ALISHA: They're stirrup pants. They have things that go around my feet.

GIRL: Like, for riding?

ALISHA: Riding what?

GIRL: Horses?

ALISHA: You're cute. I like you. Here.

ALISHA hands the GIRL a scrap of paper.

GIRL: What's this?

ALISHA: My phone number.

GIRL: Wow . . .

ALISHA: What?

GIRL: Oh, nothing.

ALISHA: You really like that number, huh?

GIRL: No. I just—

ALISHA: Are you good at math?

GIRL: Pretty good.

ALISHA: Can you help me with my division?

GIRL: Sure.

ALISHA: Don't tuck in your shirt.

GIRL: Oh, yeah.

ALISHA: I'll do it.

ALISHA fusses with the GIRL's clothes.

SYNCHRONIZED SWIMMER 1: Alisha teaches the Girl how to dress.

ALISHA: It's better when it hangs out.

SYNCHRONIZED SWIMMER 2: How to smoke Camels.

The GIRL chokes on the smoke from a cigarette.

SYNCHRONIZED SWIMMER 3: How to flirt.

SYNCHRONIZED SWIMMER 4: How to use a tampon.

ALISHA: Are you putting it in the right way?

GIRL: Yeah . . . ?

ALISHA: You have to push your finger in a little, too.

The GIRL whimpers.

Are you doing it?

GIRL: There's blood everywhere.

ALISHA: I'll do it.

GIRL: Are you sure?

ALISHA: I can't take any more of your whining.

ALISHA laughs.

GIRL: What?

ALISHA: Nothing.

GIRL: What?!?

ALISHA: You don't have any pubic hair.

GIRL: Yeah, I do . . .

ALISHA: Don't be embarrassed, sweetie. It's cute. It's like a baby bird . . .

GIRL: Shut up.

ALISHA: A dead baby bird . . .

GIRL: Yeah, and you probably have a nest.

ALISHA: Snap!

GIRL: It just stays in there?

ALISHA: Take it out in a few hours, or sooner if it gets soaked. We should make spaghetti!

SYNCHRONIZED SWIMMER 2: Alisha goes to an underage dance club called Tremors and knows how to dance really well with boys.

SYNCHRONIZED SWIMMER 3: She teaches the Girl how to dance.

SYNCHRONIZED SWIMMER 2: How to put on makeup.

SYNCHRONIZED SWIMMER 1: How to draw penises.

ALISHA: Dicks!

SYNCHRONIZED SWIMMER 1: How to draw dicks.

ALISHA and the GIRL draw cartoon penises. The SYNCHRONIZED SWIMMERS take them and hang them all over the walls.

ALISHA: You've never even kissed a guy, have you?

GIRL: Yeah . . .

ALISHA: It's okay if you haven't.

GIRL: I have.

ALISHA: Who?

GIRL: A guy.

ALISHA: Who?

GIRL: Back in Victoria.

ALISHA: What's his name?

GIRL: I don't know.

ALISHA: You don't know his name?

GIRL: He was just a guy—a guy I met on a golf course with my parents.

ALISHA: Your parents were there?

GIRL: Yeah.

> *Beat.*

We had sex.

ALISHA: Seriously?

GIRL: Yeah. I didn't really expect it, but as I was bending over to pick up a golf ball—he came up behind me and I was surprised, and before I knew it, we were having sex.

ALISHA: That sounds like rape.

GIRL: It wasn't rape. He was the caddy.

ALISHA: *(supportive)* Cool.

> *Beat.*

GIRL: Have you done it?

ALISHA: Yeah. With lots of guys.

GIRL: How many?

ALISHA counts on her fingers.

ALISHA: Ssss . . . even? Nine . . . ? But I'm not really interested in anyone now.

Beat.

GIRL: I like Donny.

ALISHA: Donny?

Sexy music plays as DONNY enters and struts across the stage listening to his Walkman.

SYNCHRONIZED SWIMMER 4: Donny wears his baseball cap on the back of his head like a bonnet.

SYNCHRONIZED SWIMMER 2: He tells really bad jokes and smells like teriyaki-flavoured beef jerky.

SYNCHRONIZED SWIMMER 1: Every day, Donny's dad drops him off at school in his Blue Line cab, like a celebrity. It's so cool.

SYNCHRO SWIMMER 4: If they ever got married, he could drive them everywhere . . .

SYNCHRO SWIMMER 2: And then just wait there until they were finished—

SYNCHRO SWIMMER 1: And then drive them home.

SYNCHRO SWIMMER 4: Donny has a huge bulge in his pants.

GIRL: What is that?

ALISHA: I think he stuffs a sock down there.

GIRL: One day, in homeroom, he came up behind me and pushed it into my back.

ALISHA: Seriously? Like, again from behind?

GIRL: Yeah, well, no, yeah.

> *A porn magazine is tossed on stage.* ALISHA *catches it and hands it to the* GIRL.

What's this?

ALISHA: It's a *Hustler.* I stole it from my dad.

> *They open it up and have a look.*

I like this one . . .

GIRL: What is she wearing?

ALISHA: A kilt.

GIRL: Yeah, but why is she so oily?

ALISHA: Guys like it. Let's choose which ones look most like us.

SYNCHRONIZED SWIMMER 2: They flip through the whole magazine.

SYNCHRONIZED SWIMMER 1: One woman's in a fire station bending over—bare-assed, holding a hose.

SYNCHRONIZED SWIMMER 2: One sips tea in a frilly white blouse and sun hat—naked from the waist down.

SYNCHRONIZED SWIMMER 4: A cheerleader with one boob exposed eats an ice cream that is half melted and dripping onto her chest.

SYNCHRONIZED SWIMMER 1: One's got giant implants with copy reading "naturally gifted."

GIRL: I would give anything to look like that.

SYNCHRONIZED SWIMMER 2: An eye?

GIRL: Yes.

SYNCHRONIZED SWIMMER 1: A foot?

GIRL: Maybe.

SYNCHRONIZED SWIMMER 4: An organ?

GIRL: As long as it wasn't a vital one. Because what's a girl without girl parts?

ALISHA: But look, see? None of *these* women have nests . . .

Scene 10.5

A musical underscore plays, reminiscent of "Part of Your World" from Disney's The Little Mermaid. *The SYNCHRONIZED SWIMMERS hang strings with pornographic images clipped to them.*

SYNCHRONIZED SWIMMER 4: They choose a secret place in the forest.

SYNCHRONIZED SWIMMER 1: They tear out pictures from the porn mag.

SYNCHRONIZED SWIMMER 2: And hang them from strings with rainbow-coloured paper clips.

ALISHA: Our very own Playboy Mansion.

SYNCHRONIZED SWIMMER 4: They lie down and look up at the goddesses whose parts are proudly exposed, their eyes seducing and inviting them into a secret world.

ALISHA: Look at her . . .

GIRL: That's me.

Scene 11

We hear a phone ringing as the WOMAN enters.

WOMAN: I need your help! I screwed up.

SYNCHRONIZED SWIMMER 5: Who are *you*?

WOMAN: Jesus!

GIRL: Relax!

WOMAN: Who are they?

GIRL: They're . . . they're my friends.

WOMAN: Well, I've never met them before.

GIRL: They usually disappear when you show up . . .

WOMAN: This isn't good. I'm getting worse.

SYNCHRONIZED SWIMMER 3: Is that your mom?

WOMAN: No!

GIRL: She's—

WOMAN: I'm her!

GIRL: But I'm not *her*.

WOMAN: *(taken aback)* You're me.

GIRL: But I'm not you. Not yet. Thank god.

WOMAN: *(seeing the cartoon penises)* What the hell is this?

The WOMAN starts tearing them down.

GIRL: Hey!

The GIRL steps in to gather up the drawings.

WOMAN: *(to the GIRL)* I did a bad thing.

SYNCHRONIZED SWIMMER 2: What did you do?

WOMAN: It's none of your business!

(to the GIRL) He's going to call any minute.

SYNCHRONIZED SWIMMER 4: Who?

WOMAN: Nobody!!

(to the GIRL) It's my fault—

SYNCHRONIZED SWIMMER 3: Why is she lying?

WOMAN: What do I do?

SYNCHRONIZED SWIMMER 2: What's the secret?

SYNCHRONIZED SWIMMER 4: Yeah.

SYNCHRONIZED SWIMMER 3: What did you do?

WOMAN: Shut the fuck up!

SYNCHRONIZED SWIMMERS: *(overlapping)* Whoa.

That is—

I can't believe you just said that . . .

That is so . . .

Why would you say that?

WOMAN: *(to the GIRL)* I texted him.

SYNCHRONIZED SWIMMER 3: "Tested him"?

WOMAN: No, "texted." I *texted* . . .

SYNCHRONIZED SWIMMER 3: "Texted."

WOMAN: It's like leaving an email—

SYNCHRONIZED SWIMMER 3: Email?

WOMAN: Forget it. I *paged* him, okay? I told him that we should meet.

SYNCHRONIZED SWIMMERS: Oooh . . .

WOMAN: It's not like that.

The WOMAN's phone rings.

SYNCHRONIZED SWIMMER 3: Oh my god, what is that?

The WOMAN pulls the phone out of her back pocket.

What *is* that?

WOMAN: *(to the GIRL)* It's him.

SYNCHRONIZED SWIMMER 4: It's a flashlight!

GIRL: Answer it!

WOMAN: What?

GIRL: Answer it!

WOMAN: I don't want to.

The SYNCHRONIZED SWIMMERS grab at the phone as the WOMAN attempts to evade them.

SYNCHRONIZED SWIMMERS: *(overlapping)* What is it?

A computer?

How do you answer it?

It's so tiny and flat!

Somehow, in the scuffle, the phone is answered.

TY: *(voice-over)* Hello?

Dead quiet as they listen to TY's *voice coming through the phone.*

Princess? It's Ty. You there?

GIRL: Yes. Say yes!

WOMAN: Yes. Hi.

TY: *(voice-over)* What you up to?

WOMAN: Uh, nothing. Just here with some—friends, or— *(fading out)* Um . . .

TY: *(voice-over)* Hello?

WOMAN: Sorry, this feels a little weird.

TY: *(voice-over)* No kidding.

WOMAN: It's been a long time.

TY: *(voice-over)* You haven't changed.

WOMAN: I still look thirteen?

TY: *(voice-over)* Nah . . . You're still pretty.

The SYNCHRONIZED SWIMMERS *shriek and giggle. A few follow the* WOMAN *off stage.*

Scene 12

The GIRL's BROTHER enters. SYNCHRONIZED SWIMMER 3 watches from the shadows.

BROTHER: You shouldn't be having any contact with boys, besides kissing.

SYNCHRONIZED SWIMMER 3: The Girl's brother had just finished reading *The Second Sex* by Simone de Beauvoir and was now pacing back and forth in the TV room.

BROTHER: That time will come when you're a *woman*. And if they dump you for not doing it?

GIRL: Doing what?

BROTHER: You know that that's all that they wanted in the first place.

(reading from the book) "No one is more arrogant toward women, more aggressive or scornful, than the man who is anxious about his virility."

The GIRL nods.

It's not just a *game*.

The GIRL shakes her head.

It's not *fun*.

The GIRL shakes her head.

It is a loving, *expressive* act between two *married* people—if not *married*, two *adults* in *love*—any other way and it loses its beauty, it's *ugly*.

The GIRL *nods, then shakes her head again . . .*

It takes away from your strength, dignity, and spirituality when given to some *teenage* boy.

SYNCHRONIZED SWIMMER 3: What her brother didn't say is that he had lost his virginity at a keg party when *he* was fourteen.

GIRL: Do you think that I'm pretty?

BROTHER: Why are you . . . ? That doesn't matter.

GIRL: Do you think that a guy could ever fall in love with me? Am I pretty enough?

BROTHER: I'm not going to respond to that.

GIRL: Why, because I'm ugly?

BROTHER: You have beautiful skin because it covers your whole body, and the amazing thing about your face is that it has two holes in it for eyes. Some people have none.

GIRL: I don't know why you can't say anything nice about me.

Scene 13

ALISHA enters.

ALISHA: What are you doing Friday night? You should tell your parents that you're sleeping over and then come with me to Tremors.

GIRL: I don't know, Alisha . . .

ALISHA: Donny will be there.

GIRL: I'll ask my parents.

ALISHA exits as the GIRL's MOM enters folding laundry.

Scene 14

MOM: No.

GIRL: Mom, I'm going to be a pretty boring person if all I do is swimming and homework.

MOM: Boring, but healthy and smart . . .

GIRL: But why?

MOM: You're not old enough.

GIRL: It's an *underage* dance club.

MOM: Sweetie, you have practice tomorrow.

GIRL: I have practice every day.

The GIRL storms off.

MOM: Where are you going?

GIRL: I'm going to bed!

MOM: It's seven o'clock.

GIRL: What am I going to do?? Hang out with *you* all night?

DAD: *(musically from off stage)* We could play Boggle, Balderdash . . .

GIRL: Dad!! Word games suck.

MOM: Language, honey. Language.

MOM exits.

Scene 15

The SYNCHRONIZED SWIMMERS enter.

SYNCHRONIZED SWIMMER 1: The Girl's room is on the top floor of the house.

SYNCHRONIZED SWIMMER 4: The only way out is through a window.

SYNCHRONIZED SWIMMER 1: She opens her swimming kit and applies waterproof makeup.

SYNCHRONIZED SWIMMER 4: Smears gel through her hair, but it droops in clumps, so she ties it back.

SYNCHRONIZED SWIMMER 1: She wears stirrup pants.

SYNCHRONIZED SWIMMER 4: Her sister's high heels are too big, so she puts on thick socks.

SYNCHRONIZED SWIMMER 1: She opens the window and lets her legs dangle out.

SYNCHRONIZED SWIMMER 4: It's a long way down.

The GIRL jumps.

Nineties hip hop plays.

Scene 16

Tremors Nightclub. The SYNCHRONIZED SWIMMERS *dance in a sexually suggestive choreographed routine, like an Ariana Grande video.*

SYNCHRONIZED SWIMMER 2: The Girl searches for Alisha.

SYNCHRONIZED SWIMMER 1: As she moves through the crowd.

SYNCHRONIZED SWIMMER 2: Through flashing lights and bobbing heads.

SYNCHRONIZED SWIMMER 4: And cigarette smoke.

SYNCHRONIZED SWIMMER 1: Older boys watch as the girls move slowly up and down.

SYNCHRONIZED SWIMMER 2: Turning like corkscrews.

SYNCHRONIZED SWIMMER 4: And then—

SYNCHRONIZED SWIMMER 2: And then—

SYNCHRONIZED SWIMMER 4: And then—

SYNCHRONIZED SWIMMER 2: She sees them.

GIRL: Donny!

SYNCHRONIZED SWIMMER 1: And Alisha.

GIRL: Alisha?

SYNCHRONIZED SWIMMER 2: And Donny.

GIRL: Tonguing each other at the back of the bar?

ALISHA and DONNY make out.

Sound and lights shift.

ALISHA: Don't be upset! I don't even like him.

GIRL: Really? You seem like you do.

ALISHA: No, really, I don't.

GIRL: Then why would you . . . ?

ALISHA: In a weird way, I was trying to make him interested in you.

Beat.

It started in class—I'd write him little notes and he'd write back. But then I squeezed his butt one day, as a test, and it backfired. I could tell that he was getting into me, so I told him to come out tonight so that I could get him into you, and then we were dancing, and he started feeling me up, so I slipped him the tongue, just to see . . . but he's a bad kisser. Which probably makes him a bad fuck. He's not worth your time.

Beat.

Say something.

Beat.

GIRL: Is it a sock?

ALISHA: No. I think it's a rolled-up face towel. And trust me, there isn't anything else down there.

Beat.

Are you upset?

GIRL: No.

SYNCHRONIZED SWIMMER 1: She isn't upset. She never actually *liked* Donny.

SYNCHRONIZED SWIMMER 2: She just liked that he was there to like.

SYNCHRONIZED SWIMMER 3: In the same way that Alisha only fucked Donny because he was there to fuck.

SYNCHRONIZED SWIMMER 1: In the same way that Donny's into Alisha because she's willing to touch his face towel.

SYNCHRONIZED SWIMMER 2: Nobody *likes* anyone.

SYNCHRONIZED SWIMMER 4: Not in a *deep* sense.

SYNCHRO SWIMMER 3: It's just anyone who happens to be there.

TY enters.

TY: Hey there, princess.

Transition.

Scene 17

The GIRL and the SYNCHRONIZED SWIMMERS are gone. The WOMAN, now in a dress and makeup, stands opposite TY in the food court of the Rideau Centre.

TY: You look good, girl.

WOMAN: Thanks. You too.

TY: Thanks, baby.

WOMAN: No problem . . . *man.*

TY: Haha! Can you believe this place? All fancy now? Like you.

WOMAN: Uh huh.

TY: Man!

WOMAN: Baby!

TY: Yeah?

WOMAN: No. I was just saying "man!" "baby!" "manbaby."

TY is confused.

Maybe we should sit down.

TY: You don't want to get something?

WOMAN: No.

TY: Fries or a Coke? Fancy salad?

WOMAN: No.

They sit down.

So.

TY: You got kids?

WOMAN: Kids? No.

TY: I got two.

He takes out his wallet and shows her.

That's Izzy and Racer. Look, matching sweaters. Cute little fuckers.

WOMAN: Uh huh.

TY: That your boyfriend?

The WOMAN turns to look.

The other day? When we—

WOMAN: Oh, yeah. Paul. That's my boyfriend. I—

TY: He know you're here?

Beat.

WOMAN: No.

TY: Shit . . .

Beat.

WOMAN: You sound different.

TY: Yeah?

WOMAN: The way you speak. You don't have that . . . that way of—

TY: Oh yeah, I got it treated. It's called "cluttering." When you clump all your words together, like in the alphabet: h, i, j, k, lmnop. Speeds up like that. Or slows down: w . . . x . . . y / and—

WOMAN: Mm . . .

TY: Changesalltime. See? There it is.

WOMAN: Okay.

TY: It change. Chang-*es*—

WOMAN: Got it.

TY: There we go, sometimes I just have to—

WOMAN: I'd like to talk about what happened between us.

TY: What happened?

WOMAN: Twenty-five years ago.

TY: *(rapidly)* Whatyouwanttotalkabout?

WOMAN: How it affected, how I was aff—

TY: Infected?

WOMAN: Aaa . . . ffected. I'm still affected by that time in my life—

TY: Okay . . . like, in a good way?

WOMAN: Is that a joke?

TY: No.

WOMAN: No?

TY: No?

> *Beat.*

WOMAN: I'd like to hear your side of the story.

TY: Okay . . . like now?

WOMAN: Yeah, like now.

TY: Like, out loud?

WOMAN: Yeah. Tell me about the kid you had sex with.

TY: Huh? What?

WOMAN: I'd like to know what you remember.

TY: Remember? I don't . . . / remember.

WOMAN: *(firmly)* Okay, well, let me *remind* you, then. About what *happened.*

TY: Why are you so upset?

WOMAN: I'm not upset.

TY: Emph-sizing yer words and shit. Emph—

WOMAN: Why don't I give you my side of the story. Maybe that will get the wheels turning?

Scene 18

The Rec Centre. The GIRL and her MOM enter.

GIRL: Mom! I have to go! I have to get in the pool!

MOM: We're early!

GIRL: Coach Cindy says we have to be wet and warm five minutes before practice even starts, otherwise she freaks out. I've got to go!

MOM: I just wanted to say ... *(quieter)* I think we should go bra shopping this week.

GIRL: What?

MOM: I think that we should go bra—

GIRL: Mom, why are you whispering? You said I didn't need one.

MOM: Well, I've thought about it, and I know there's nothing really there / yet—

GIRL: Mom!

MOM: But I think that it will make it a little easier to fit in, even if it's just for decoration.

GIRL: Do we have to talk about this now?

MOM: I'll stay and watch, and we can talk after.

GIRL: No, no, no! It's private practice today.

MOM: Private?

GIRL: Or, like, Coach Cindy said no parents. You're not allowed. You get in the way. Bye! I'll bus home. You don't need to pick me up.

The GIRL turns to leave.

MOM: Don't I get a kiss?

The GIRL quickly kisses her MOM.

Transition.

Scene 19

COACH CINDY: There are only girls at the Rec Centre today, so the Girl hides in the boys' washroom.

A door creaks open. High heels clack on the floor, as if in an echoing chamber. The GIRL hugs her legs to her chest and holds her breath. COACH CINDY takes the stall next to her.

You won't be making practice today?

Long pause.

GIRL: I don't feel well. I think I need to go to the doctor.

COACH CINDY: I don't think that you'll find one in the boys' washroom.

COACH CINDY reads graffiti on the stall door.

Oh.

Beat.

"Sophie Sucks Dick."

GIRL: Pardon?

COACH CINDY: "Emily's a pathetic ho."

GIRL: I—

COACH CINDY: "For a good time call . . . " Oh. It's been scratched out. Probably by some well-meaning janitor . . . Darn. I like to come in here before practice . . . to clear my mind.

> *There is a click of a lighter.*

Don't tell the other girls. It's exciting to have secrets. No matter how old you are.

> *COACH CINDY inhales deeply and sighs.*

How old am I, do you think?

> *Beat.*

Take a guess.

GIRL: Thhhirty . . . ffffive?

COACH CINDY: That's nice . . . No, I've been around a lot longer than that. Not gonna put too fine a point on it, but I'm up into the three digits. I grew up fast. Way too fast. It was my butterfly stroke. They'd never seen anything like me. It's a curse really. All I did was train, train, train—never mind what I thought and felt—and that was it for my childhood. And once it's gone, it's gone *forever*. I know you look at me with my fitted track pants and nail polish, and my medals, and these tits.

My god . . . these tits. They're not real. None of it's real. The only thing that keeps me looking this good is you girls. Your devotion to the team, your spirit . . . it feeds me. That's what I try to capture in my routines. All that *life*. Youth, it's so . . . powerful. But you're going to skip practice today.

GIRL: No, I wasn't—

COACH CINDY: It's okay. You can't get out of here without my permission.

GIRL: It's not like I'm skipping. I have a doctor's appointment.

COACH CINDY: Oh yeah? You got a slip with a signature from Mommy on it?

GIRL: No.

COACH CINDY: Didn't think so.

GIRL: Do I need one? I really can't swim today. I'm not feeling—

COACH CINDY: *You don't need to make excuses.* Some days you just can't. Some days you gotta say, "Screw it. Screw you people."

GIRL: No—

COACH CINDY: "I've been doing what you want my whole fucking life. I'm thirteen years old, I'm gonna do what I want."

The GIRL considers this.

Of course, you do something once, and it's easier to do it again, and it's a slippery slope . . . But that's the grown-up in me talking.

Beat.

Oh, here's an interesting one:

(reading) "Coach Cindy give good bone." Hm, cryptic. I think I'm going to correct that.

She writes on the stall.

"Coach Cindy give good *advice*." That's better. You still there?

GIRL: Uh huh.

COACH CINDY: I say, *do what you want.* Follow your heart's desire. I mean, what's one practice?

GIRL: Okay . . . so, like, I have your permission?

COACH CINDY: Of course. But I'll need something in exchange.

GIRL: Oh.

COACH CINDY: Promise you'll stay on my team.

GIRL: I wasn't going to quit or anything.

COACH CINDY: You're not going to quit?

GIRL: No.

COACH CINDY: You're going to stay on my team. Say it.

GIRL: I'm going to stay on your team.

COACH CINDY: Good. You have my permission. Hit it, girls!

COACH CINDY exits.

Scene 20

SYNCHRONIZED SWIMMER 2: The Girl takes the number fourteen—

SYNCHRONIZED SWIMMER 4: Then transfers to the eighty-seven—

SYNCHRONIZED SWIMMER 2: Gets off at the Mac's Milk.

SYNCHRONIZED SWIMMER 1: But he isn't there—

SYNCHRONIZED SWIMMER 2: So she calls him from a pay phone.

TY: *(voice-over)* Where are you?

SYNCHRONIZED SWIMMER 1: He says.

TY: *(voice-over)* Okay, wait there a minute.

SYNCHRONIZED SWIMMER 4: He says.

SYNCHRONIZED SWIMMER 2: She waits.

SYNCHRONIZED SWIMMER 1: A guy walks past her wearing a tank top, even though it's forty below.

SYNCHRONIZED SWIMMER 2: A woman smokes out a second-floor window.

SYNCHRONIZED SWIMMER 4: A dog lunges at her.

SYNCHRONIZED SWIMMER 1: Then Ty comes skipping around the corner.

The SYNCHRONIZED SWIMMERS take a collective breath in.

TY: Hey, princess.

GIRL: Hi!

Beat.

TY: *(stringing words together)* Caughtthebusokay?

GIRL: What?

TY: Thebusokayyoucaughtdownatthecorner?

GIRL: Sorry. Still not—

TY: Catchtheeightyseven?

GIRL: Huh?

TY: *(spelling it out)* The *eighty-seven bus.*

GIRL: Yeah.

TY whistles tunelessly and does a little freestyle rapping.

Scene 21

SYNCHRONIZED SWIMMER 4: Ty takes the Girl into a semi-detached house.

We see the figure of ZACH.

SYNCHRONIZED SWIMMER 1: Where some guy named Zach sits—

SYNCHRONIZED SWIMMER 4: Rolling a joint.

SYNCHRONIZED SWIMMER 2: Long arms.

SYNCHRONIZED SWIMMER 1: Smooth.

SYNCHRONIZED SWIMMER 2: Shiny.

SYNCHRONIZED SWIMMER 4: He looks at the Girl.

SYNCHRONIZED SWIMMER 1: He laughs.

ZACH laughs.

SYNCHRONIZED SWIMMER 2: Music videos play on a TV.

SYNCHRONIZED SWIMMER 1: Women in thongs.

SYNCHRONIZED SWIMMER 4: Strong bodies.

SYNCHRONIZED SWIMMER 1: Bending.

SYNCHRONIZED SWIMMER 2: Shaking.

SYNCHRONIZED SWIMMER 4: Gyrating.

SYNCHRONIZED SWIMMER 1: She stares harder at the TV.

TY: Come with me.

TY leads the GIRL to another area of the stage and the SYNCHRONIZED SWIMMERS follow.

Scene 22

SYNCHRONIZED SWIMMER 5: He takes her hand and leads her to a room.

SYNCHRONIZED SWIMMER 3: A room with nothing in it.

SYNCHRONIZED SWIMMER 4: No posters.

SYNCHRONIZED SWIMMER 1: No pictures.

SYNCHRONIZED SWIMMER 2: No clock.

SYNCHRONIZED SWIMMER 5: Just a mattress on the floor.

SYNCHRONIZED SWIMMER 1: And a crumpled sheet on top.

GIRL & SYNCHRONIZED SWIMMERS: You live here?

SYNCHRONIZED SWIMMER 2: She asks.

SYNCHRONIZED SWIMMER 1: He sits down and pats the mattress beside him.

SYNCHRONIZED SWIMMER 3: She sits down.

TY: You smoke?

GIRL & SYNCHRONIZED SWIMMERS: Yeah.

SYNCHRONIZED SWIMMER 3: He lights a joint.

SYNCHRONIZED SWIMMER 5: Not that kind of smoking.

SYNCHRONIZED SWIMMER 4: He passes it to her and she takes a hit, and then he starts taking his shirt off.

SYNCHRONIZED SWIMMER 2: Then tries to remove hers.

GIRL & SYNCHRONIZED SWIMMERS: No . . .

TY: Why not?

GIRL & SYNCHRONIZED SWIMMERS: Because.

TY: You're just gonna sit there?

GIRL & SYNCHRONIZED SWIMMERS: That's as far as I want to go.

TY: Really.

SYNCHRONIZED SWIMMER 4: He keeps going.

GIRL & SYNCHRONIZED SWIMMERS: I'm a virgin.

  TY laughs.

What?

TY: I can't believe it.

SYNCHRONIZED SWIMMER 5: He looks at her. A bedroom stare.

SYNCHRONIZED SWIMMER 4: He moves closer to her face.

SYNCHRONIZED SWIMMER 3: His mouth softens.

SYNCHRONIZED SWIMMER 1: Their lips touch.

SYNCHRONIZED SWIMMER 2: She tries to keep up with what feels like—

SYNCHRONIZED SWIMMER 1: Wriggling worms. Slugs—

SYNCHRONIZED SWIMMER 4: Something alive . . .

SYNCHRONIZED SWIMMER 3: His lips taste like the earth.

SYNCHRONIZED SWIMMER 1: Like the inside of a cardboard box.

SYNCHRONIZED SWIMMER 3: She imagines she's someone else.

SYNCHRONIZED SWIMMER 4: She thinks about Donny.

SYNCHRONIZED SWIMMER 1: Her sister and that guy in the church parking lot.

SYNCHRONIZED SWIMMER 5: She imagines she's one of those sex goddesses from the magazine.

SYNCHRONIZED SWIMMER 4: Someone beautiful.

SYNCHRONIZED SWIMMER 1: Someone fully developed.

SYNCHRONIZED SWIMMER 4: Someone he'd want.

SYNCHRONIZED SWIMMER 2: A "real" woman.

SYNCHRONIZED SWIMMER 3: Then he looks at her.

SYNCHRONIZED SWIMMER 4: And she realizes that he'll have sex with her, whether she wants to or not.

SYNCHRONIZED SWIMMER 2: She doesn't want her first time to be rape.

SYNCHRONIZED SWIMMER 1: So she takes her top off.

SYNCHRONIZED SWIMMER 3: And he smiles.

SYNCHRONIZED SWIMMER 1: He laughs.

GIRL & SYNCHRONIZED SWIMMERS: What?

TY & SYNCHRONIZED SWIMMERS: Nothing.

GIRL: Why are you smiling?

TY: I'm lucky.

Scene 23

A telephone conversation between the GIRL *and* ALISHA *plays as the* GIRL *gets up out of bed and retraces her steps back home.*

GIRL: *(voice-over)* Alisha. We did it. We had sex.

ALISHA: *(voice-over)* I thought you were at practice.

GIRL: *(voice-over)* Yeah, I skipped.

Beat.

(voice-over) I did it.

ALISHA: *(voice-over)* Did what?

GIRL: *(voice-over)* With Ty.

ALISHA: *(voice-over)* Oh no . . .

GIRL: *(voice-over)* What?

Beat.

(voice-over) Alisha, what?

ALISHA: *(voice-over)* Don't ever go back there. They're bad people.

COACH CINDY: When the Girl gets home, she will race up to the bathroom. She will remove her clothes and stare at her naked form in the mirror, searching for what impression the day's events have made on her body. An irreversible change. Her "parts" now have greater *significance*. She puts on her flannel nightgown, huddles into bed with her favourite teddy, and dreams of a storm fast approaching.

Water showers down on the GIRL.

Intermission.

Act 2

Scene 1

Back in the food court, the WOMAN *scarfs down a mega-size serving of tater tots.*

WOMAN: *(mid-sentence)* And then, what was it . . . a week, a week and a half ago? I was riding my bike and one of my shopping bags got caught in the front wheel and I flew over the handlebars. And, as I'm lying there on the pavement, gasping for air, wondering if I've broken my ribs, these random men start swarming me. A police officer, a construction worker, and I'm thinking: What is this? The Village People?

"Ma'am?"

I feel like I've punctured a lung.

"Should we call an ambulance? Ma'am? Are you okay? Ma'am?"

Yes! I'm fine! Jesus! What do you want from me, a *hand job*?

TY: You said that?

> *Beat.*

WOMAN: Then I shredded my fingers on a mandoline.

TY: Like, a little guitar?

WOMAN: No, like, to cut vegetables. "Fancy" vegetables.

TY: Oh.

WOMAN: It doesn't matter. The point is, there was a lot of blood. Like, a lot. And I thought, I literally thought: "I should just shove my hands into a blender and put them out of their misery."

TY: Shit.

WOMAN: Um, what else? Stubbing my toes, burning my fingers, oh, and this—on my neck.

She pulls her collar down.

TY: What's that from?

WOMAN: Steaming my face over a hot pot.

TY: Oh. Like Korean . . . ?

WOMAN: No, just boiling water to open my pores. Um, so, yeah. All these "accidents." They start to feel intentional.

TY laughs uncomfortably. He's having a hard time keeping up with the thread of the conversation.

Like coming here. Why am I here? Maybe on some level I want to "open the wound." I don't know, it's like my body just does stuff before my mind has a chance to catch up. Why did I get involved with you? I didn't even like you.

TY: You think I wanted to be with some scrawny little thing? With big bushy eyebrows and braces? Flat chest, no butt, no hips—

WOMAN: Okay . . .

TY: No, no, no, listen. I have flat feet. So? My friends tease me about it, but fuck 'em, it's none of their business.

WOMAN: Wow.

TY: We all have our own shit. Things happen. The world kicks the shit out of you. When I write, it's all backwards and shit.

WOMAN: I'm sorry—

TY: When I speak, for years, no one could understand me.

WOMAN: That has nothing to do with me. I didn't make it so you couldn't speak. I didn't do fucked-up shit / to you—

TY: It was just sex.

WOMAN: Well, I didn't want it.

TY: Then whydidwedoit—why did we do it, like, three times that day?

WOMAN: We didn't.

TY: We did. And then you took off.

WOMAN: Oh, okay, so now you remember? / You remember the whole—

TY: I mean, like, that hurts. Like, like, it would have been nice to at least talkafter. *Talk.* Smoke a joint.

WOMAN: Are you joking?

TY: You took off!

WOMAN: I went home. I had a curfew. I sat at the dinner table and ate fish sticks with my parents.

Scene 2

MOM and DAD enter and speak to the GIRL.

MOM: You look pale. Honey?

DAD: Huh?

MOM: Don't you think she looks wan?

DAD: How's my angel? Tired from all that swimming?

MOM: Her bones are still growing. Drink your milk.

GIRL: I'm not hungry. I need to lie down.

WOMAN: I was a mess. I meet this man, and the next day he's fucking me on a stained mattress in his buddy's apartment.

TY: Wait, wait. You ain't remembering right.

The GIRL has opened her diary and is reading.

GIRL: Dear Future Me—

TY: You're making it sound like one night we met, the next day we fucked. It didn't happen that way.

GIRL: There's so much going on here, where do I begin?

WOMAN: It did.

TY: No, we were dating before that happened. You'd come to the mall, you'd order Yogen Früz, we were hanging around . . . So it's not like I'm some kind of sex predator or something.

GIRL: First of all, I met a boy.

The WOMAN and TY turn to the GIRL.

WOMAN: Boy?

GIRL: Well, he's twenty-one.

TY: *(to the WOMAN)* We were dating.

WOMAN: *(looking at the GIRL)* I don't remember it that way.

GIRL: He just called me and asked when my spare is tomorrow. I said 10:50, and he said he's going to pick me up at school.

WOMAN: *(to TY)* We weren't "dating."

TY: *(to the WOMAN)* What would you call it, then?

WOMAN: *(to TY)* Raped? Molested? Taken advantage of?

GIRL: I feel so special.

The WOMAN and TY turn to watch the GIRL.

He's supposed to be a stud who fucks around with a lot of girls, but he isn't.

I know I sound a little naive but he's really sweet. Today, he came to my synchro practice—all the girls knew about him coming but most of them assumed that he was my age, and when they saw Ty and his really nasty face, they looked so taken aback. Alisha said she overheard Jake and Ty talking. Jake asked him, "Have you fucked her yet?" And Ty said he wanted to "take this one slow . . . " Wow! He also said that he doesn't care if we don't have sex for three years, he just wants to be with me. I am very happy.

The SISTER storms in and the WOMAN and TY exit.

Scene 3

SISTER: What are you doing? You're taking forever! I need to get ready!

GIRL: Sorry.

SISTER: What's with you? You're spending hours in here. Did you use my hair dryer?

GIRL: No.

SISTER: Then why is there hand cream all over it? Are you okay? You look like a ghost eel.

GIRL: Thanks.

SISTER: And don't use my conditioner! It's expensive. And I need it for my shitty hair!

The GIRL observes her SISTER getting ready.

What are you staring at, perv?

GIRL: Are you meeting that guy?

SISTER: What guy?

GIRL: From the parking lot.

SISTER: His name's Doug.

GIRL: Are you in love?

SISTER: Shut up.

GIRL: Are you?

SISTER: I guess.

GIRL: What does it feel like?

SISTER: *(softening)* I don't know . . . At first it's like you're just drawn to the person, like, even if you don't really know why. Even though he's kind of weird and you hate his lime-green cargo pants. And it's weird because you feel awkward and stupid, but you keep going back and then you start *doing things* together and suddenly you're spending way more time with him than anyone else, and that's sort of weird, cuz you start thinking way more about what he's thinking and what he needs than what you're thinking or what you need. And the rest of the world just falls away and then, one day, you can't believe it but you ask him if you can borrow his lime-green cargo pants.

GIRL: I think I might be in love.

SISTER: What, with your Ken doll?

Scene 4

COACH CINDY enters blowing a whistle. The SYNCHRONIZED SWIMMERS strut out in formation and begin a routine. The GIRL joins them.

GIRL: Either I'm in love or I'm sex crazy. Like my grandma.

SYNCHRONIZED SWIMMER 2: Your grandma?

COACH CINDY: Straight backs! Long necks! Not aggressive! *Baby* swans!

GIRL: My uncle Ricky told me that she waited for grandpa every night to come home from work.

SYNCHRONIZED SWIMMER 2: So?

COACH CINDY: Soft and lovely. Sweet and pure. Sexy and strong.

GIRL: The sound of his car in the driveway would set her "writhing in her chair."

COACH CINDY: Ruffling feathers! Ruffling feathers!

GIRL: Like Pavlov's dog.

SYNCHRONIZED SWIMMER 4: Whatever that means.

GIRL: It means she was sex crazy! That's what he called it. Sex crazy. So maybe it's possible that she passed it down to me, like, genetically. Maybe I can't control it, maybe being sex crazy is, like, a family trait.

Scene 5

MOM, ALISHA, and the GIRL's BROTHER enter and speak to the GIRL.

MOM: What's wrong?

ALISHA: What's wrong?

BROTHER: What's wrong?

GIRL: Nothing. Nothing's wrong.

BROTHER: Then why are you acting like a brat?

MOM: Are you having some trouble transitioning?

ALISHA: You're so quiet.

GIRL: *(to ALISHA)* Do you think that I should get some birth control?

BROTHER: The school called.

ALISHA: I wouldn't do that if I were you . . .

BROTHER: You're falling behind in math.

GIRL: Really?

MOM: You seem a bit off.

ALISHA: You really think you're going to be doing it more?

GIRL: I don't know, maybe.

BROTHER: You need to grow up.

ALISHA: "Maybe"?

BROTHER: Don't you think it's time to take some responsibility?

MOM: Are you low in iron? Sweetie?

GIRL: Well, yeah, probably.

BROTHER: Then stop with the hanging out.

ALISHA: With Ty?

MOM: We'll get you some ground beef.

BROTHER: Stop with the secrets.

ALISHA: You can tell me.

BROTHER: Mom and Dad are worried sick.

MOM: We'll have a burger night.

GIRL: Yeah . . .

ALISHA: They'll make you fat.

GIRL: Really?

ALISHA: And if you forget to take them, you bleed, for like thirty days straight.

BROTHER: It's time to think about others for a change.

The GIRL's BROTHER and ALISHA exit.

MOM: Honey.

GIRL: Huh?

MOM: Are you listening?

GIRL: I'm listening.

MOM: We could go to the Gatineaus. Have a walk around the lake.

GIRL: I don't feel like it.

MOM: But you love nature!

GIRL: Sorry. Yeah, I do, I do . . .

SYNCHRONIZED SWIMMER 5: But she also loves cigarettes.

SYNCHRONIZED SWIMMER 2: And skipping school.

SYNCHRONIZED SWIMMER 5: Hitching free rides with cabbies in the dead of winter.

TY: After you, princess.

SYNCHRONIZED SWIMMER 5: He says.

SYNCHRONIZED SWIMMER 4: And she feels a warm gust of air up her skirt.

SYNCHRONIZED SWIMMER 2: As they step into the Rideau Centre.

GIRL: Like royalty.

SYNCHRONIZED SWIMMER 4: Her heart races as she rides down the escalator.

SYNCHRONIZED SWIMMER 5: Shoeshiners sit on thrones looking over everything.

SYNCHRONIZED SWIMMER 2: The chatter. The chicken grease.

SYNCHRONIZED SWIMMER 4: The fluorescent lights!

GIRL: Manchu Wok!

Scene 6

DONNY and BEN enter. DONNY still has the face towel in his pants.

DONNY: *(whispering)* Hey! Hey!

GIRL: Hi, Donny. Hi, Ben.

DONNY: What does a beaver smell like?

GIRL: A beaver? I don't—

DONNY: Fish!

BEN laughs his head off.

GIRL: Okay, whatever.

DONNY: Get it?

GIRL: Yeah, I get it. And you smell like beef jerky.

BEN: Whoa!

DONNY: Like what?

DONNY sniffs his armpits.

BEN: Who's that guy you were hanging out with in the market?

GIRL: What are you talking about?

DONNY: Ben saw you with that weirdo in the market. With the ponytail?

BEN: And the pager.

DONNY: You a thing now?

GIRL: Maybe.

DONNY: Can you score us some pot?

GIRL: No. He's not a drug dealer.

BEN: Then why does he have a pager?

DONNY: And why does he hang out at the mall with teenagers all day?

BEN: Isn't he, like, twenty-three?

GIRL: Why do you even care, Donny?

DONNY: I don't care. Why would I care if you want to be a slut? Hey, what kind of shoes does a pedophile wear?

BEN: I don't know.

DONNY: White Vans!

GIRL: Oh yeah? Fuck you, you piece of shit. Try saying that to his face. Ty's street. All you do is play *Sonic the Hedgehog* and jerk off to your mother's underwear all day.

DONNY: Screw you, slut.

GIRL: Yeah, poor baby. Go, go! Go cry in your face towel!

DONNY and BEN exit.

Asshole!

Scene 7

The BOY appears holding a phone.

BOY: Hello?

The GIRL holds a phone too.

GIRL: Hey, dork.

BOY: Dinkus!

GIRL: Sorry I haven't called in a while.

BOY: It's okay.

GIRL: No, it's not. How are you?

BOY: Good. I sent you a class photo. Did you get it?

GIRL: Oh yeah. You were wearing a Swatch watch . . .

BOY: Mildred got it for me.

GIRL: Who?

BOY: My mom.

GIRL: Oh, yeah.

Beat.

BOY: How's synchro?

GIRL: Coach Cindy says that if I don't smile harder she'll draw eyebrows on my forehead.

BOY: Why?

GIRL: To match with the other girls. I don't fucking know. She's crazy. Everyone's crazy.

Beat.

Like the hall monitor. He told me to pull down my skirt today because I was "objectifying myself."

BOY: What does that mean?

GIRL: Being a slut, I guess. And then I was pulled out of class for writing notes, and my parents grounded me because they said I stole money off the kitchen counter. I just feel like barfing.

TY: Pssst!

BOY: Did you?

GIRL: *(distracted)* What?

BOY: Steal money?

TY: Pssst!

GIRL: Ty?

TY enters, soaking wet.

TY: Hey, princess.

GIRL: Oh my god.

BOY: Dinkus?

TY: Who's that?

GIRL: I gotta go.

BOY: Is that your brother?

The GIRL hangs up.

GIRL: What are you doing here? And how did you climb all the way up the side of the house?

TY: I'm high.

Beat.

What you wearing? A onesie?

GIRL: It's a nightgown.

TY: Shit's weird.

GIRL: It's Ottawa. It's freakin' cold.

TY looks around the room.

TY: I feel like I just stepped into a zoo.

GIRL: My stuffies . . .

TY: What animal's that?

GIRL: It's a walrus.

TY: Trippy.

GIRL: Why are you so jumpy?

TY: I gotta piss.

GIRL: I'll get you a bucket.

TY: I ain't pissing in no bucket.

GIRL: A yogurt container or something.

TY: Can't I use a bathroom downstairs?

GIRL: Wait! No!

TY goes downstairs.

Okay...

TY: How many rooms in this house?

GIRL: Four.

TY: Your sister in there?

GIRL: Shhh!

(pointing) That's the bathroom.

MOM: *(off stage)* Hello?

GIRL: Shit!

The GIRL and TY deke into the bathroom. The light goes out.

MOM: Honey?

The GIRL opens the door a crack. TY hides behind her.

What's going on? Are you okay?

GIRL: Yeah.

MOM: Well, get back to bed. It's late and we can hear you rambling around!

The GIRL watches her MOM go.

GIRL: *(to TY)* Hurry up!

TY: Jesus. Are those toilet roll cozies?

GIRL: What?

TY: This basket shit . . .

GIRL: You're not making any sense.

TY: Should I flush?

GIRL: NO! C'mon.

> *They sneak back up to the GIRL's room. TY does a bit of freestyle rapping.*

Shhh . . .

> *The GIRL closes the door as TY gets into her bed. She joins him.*

You stink.

TY: Well, get me a bowl of water, a face cloth, or something.

GIRL: We were just in the bathroom! I'm not going to go back down.

TY: Well, I guess I'll just stink, then. Thanks for letting me stay.

GIRL: You're welcome.

TY: I'm not sure if I'm going to be able to sleep.

> *The WOMAN storms in to interrogate TY.*

WOMAN: Excuse me.

TY: Whoa!

WOMAN: Sorry, am I interrupting?

TY: Who's—

WOMAN: What's going on here?

GIRL: What are you doing in here?

TY: Is this your—

WOMAN: I'm thirteen years old and there's a man in my bed.

GIRL: Fourteen.

WOMAN: Shut it. You were thirteen when he molested you.

(to TY) So, can you explain to me how you got here?

TY: I came in through the—

WOMAN: No, I understand. What I'm asking is what possessed you to climb up the side of my house, stoned out of your mind, in the middle of the night, to tuck in with me and my stuffies.

TY: I didn't have anywhere else to go?

WOMAN: What, are you homeless?

TY: Nah, my ma kicked me out cuz my brother and I hot-boxed the basement.

> *The WOMAN plays the following dialogue mockingly, in contrast to the GIRL's real concern.*

WOMAN & GIRL: Aw, I'm sorry.

TY: She was all screamy, so we dropped acid and hit the club, even though I'm on probation, and if anything happens and I get caught, I'm going to jail—

WOMAN & GIRL: Shit . . .

TY: —I don't have money to pay the cover, but the bouncers let me in.

WOMAN & GIRL: That's nice.

TY: I guess they don't want trouble cuz they think I'm crazy—

WOMAN & GIRL: Really?

TY: Or, like, I got a "chemical imbalance" or something, which I kinda do, cuz the lights are leaving tracers and I'm floating and everyone's looking at me, and I'm not just paranoid. Then I see this little shit at the bar who owes me money. My brother tries to stop me—but I'm strong as fuck—

WOMAN & GIRL: Yeah?

TY: —stronger than any fucker in the place. "You gonna buy me a drink?" I say to the little shit at the bar. He nods at me and reaches for his wallet, so I grab him by the throat. "What, I'm some kind of beggar to you?" Then everything goes sideways.

WOMAN & GIRL: Oh no!

TY: Lights go on, music stops, everyone's fighting, including my brother. The cops are coming and I gotta fight my way out and run, but where? Nowhere. There's only one place I can think of.

WOMAN & GIRL: Right.

TY: I had nowhere else to go.

WOMAN: Right, so you creep in here in the middle of the night?

TY: You make it sound like it was armed robbery.

WOMAN: No, it was a power trip. You wanted to be in my house, in my bedroom with my parents sleeping downstairs.

GIRL: Shhh!

WOMAN: Sorry.

TY: *(to the GIRL)* I wanted to see you.

GIRL: Just let him stay. I'll set the alarm and he'll leave before Mom and Dad wake up.

WOMAN: *(to the GIRL)* See, this is exactly why you shouldn't be making the decisions.

TY: We're just sleepin'.

WOMAN: *(to TY)* No, we had sex.

GIRL: *(to TY)* No.

TY: *(to the GIRL)* Why not?

GIRL: Cuz I don't want to.

TY: *(to the GIRL)* C'mon. Why not?

GIRL: Something's not right down there.

WOMAN: Fucking chlamydia!

Scene 8

ALISHA enters as TY and the WOMAN exit.

ALISHA: Whatever. I had it once. Just go to a walk-in.

GIRL: Do you have a bruise on your face?

ALISHA: No. *(then) Obviously.*

GIRL: Alisha, how did you get it?

ALISHA: I smashed it while pole dancing. I'm kidding. It's a hickey.

ALISHA notices a man lurking nearby.

Let's get out of here.

ALISHA leads the GIRL away.

GIRL: Who's that?

ALISHA: Some guy who's been following me.

GIRL: Is he a friend of your dad's?

ALISHA: *(yelling to the man)* Not now!

GIRL: It looks like he wants you to—

ALISHA: I said, not now!

GIRL: Who is he?

ALISHA: Some perv. I need to get out of here. Can I stay at your place?

GIRL: What do you mean, like, for the night?

ALISHA: My dad kicked me out.

GIRL: You mean you can't go back at all?

ALISHA: *(realizing)* No? Okay, don't worry about it.

GIRL: No, I just—

ALISHA: Forget it. I understand.

GIRL: No, I just don't know if my parents will let you.

ALISHA: Why? Because I'm trash?

GIRL: No. Because of homework and chores and bedtime . . . They're super strict right now.

ALISHA: Come with me.

GIRL: I can't.

ALISHA: Please . . .

GIRL: I need to get home.

ALISHA: Come. I need to be with someone.

SYNCHRONIZED SWIMMER 4: They head to the forest behind the Girl's house. Alisha is quiet during their walk.

SYNCHRONIZED SWIMMER 1: They pick cigarette butts up off the sidewalk and smoke them.

SYNCHRONIZED SWIMMER 3: It feels good to be together again. On a secret mission—

SYNCHRONIZED SWIMMER 2: To a place that only they know about.

SYNCHRONIZED SWIMMER 4: "Their very own Playboy Mansion."

SYNCHRONIZED SWIMMER 2: But when they get there . . .

SYNCHRONIZED SWIMMER 3 & 4: All of the pictures have been torn to shreds.

SYNCHRONIZED SWIMMER 1: Green moss has been ripped from the earth—

SYNCHRONIZED SWIMMER 3 & 4: Branches have been broken.

SYNCHRONIZED SWIMMER 3: Naked women gored with twigs.

SYNCHRONIZED SWIMMER 1: Maybe it was her brother?

SYNCHRONIZED SWIMMER 4: Or her dad?

SYNCHRONIZED SWIMMER 3: Donny?

SYNCHRONIZED SWIMMER 2: Or Ben?

SYNCHRONIZED SWIMMER 1: Or that crazy creep down the street who irons naked in the window?

SYNCHRONIZED SWIMMER 3 & 4: There was no way to know.

SYNCHRONIZED SWIMMER 4: And even if they did, what would they say?

GIRL: Did you destroy our porn shrine?

ALISHA: Those girls were us!

Scene 9

COACH CINDY enters with a megaphone. The SYNCHRONIZED SWIMMERS ready themselves for the team routine, stripping off their track suits.

COACH CINDY: You're not victims!

SYNCHRONIZED SWIMMERS: We're not victims!

COACH CINDY: Then what are you?

SYNCHRONIZED SWIMMERS: Strong!

COACH CINDY: Strong?

SYNCHRONIZED SWIMMERS: Fierce!

COACH CINDY: That's right.

SYNCHRONIZED SWIMMERS: Young!

COACH CINDY: My beauties.

SYNCHRONIZED SWIMMERS: Fresh!

COACH CINDY: Clean!

SYNCHRONIZED SWIMMERS: Pure!

COACH CINDY: Now smile!!

The SYNCHRONIZED SWIMMERS smile.

It's the only way to get air in.

The SYNCHRONIZED SWIMMERS *take their starting deck pose for
the team routine. Nose plugs in, they smile with mouths agape,
to get air in. They dive into the pool. The* GIRL *struggles to keep
up. Arms and legs flail around her and she becomes disoriented.
The routine ends with a hard heel to the side of her head. The*
SYNCHRONIZED SWIMMERS *get out of the pool and the* GIRL *is left
treading water.* COACH CINDY *walks out onto the diving board.*

You're struggling to keep up.

GIRL: Swimming sucks. I'm tired.

COACH CINDY: You're unfocused.

GIRL: It's too hard.

COACH CINDY: Aw . . . is it? There's a man whose been coming around
the pool. He says that he knows you. Does he?

GIRL: Does he?

COACH CINDY: Does he?

GIRL: Does he . . . ?

COACH CINDY: Know you. He says that he's your cousin. Is he?

GIRL: Is he . . . ?

COACH CINDY: Is he your cousin? Your teammates say he's a friend of
yours. Are they lying? Or are you lying?

Beat.

GIRL: He's my boyfriend.

COACH CINDY: Oh . . . what does that entail?

GIRL: He's my boyfriend. We're like, together. We're like, going out, dating, or . . . I don't know, he's my boyfriend.

COACH CINDY: Well, he wouldn't be my first choice.

GIRL: I don't want to do synchro anymore. I quit.

COACH CINDY: That's not going to happen, sweetie. See, maybe what you're not quite getting here is that the team extends well beyond the Rec Centre. I have girls who ain't in the pool at all, girls with the wrong bodies for sports. I have people on my team who can't swim or walk or even move their hands.

SHANNON appears.

SHANNON: Hi.

GIRL: Shannon?

COACH CINDY: Shannon Lishman for example. She's a girl on my team.

SYNCHRONIZED SWIMMER 1: About a month ago, Shannon stopped coming to homeroom.

SYNCHRONIZED SWIMMER 3: You didn't even notice.

GIRL: No, I, no—

SYNCHRONIZED SWIMMER 5: Partly because she didn't want to.

GIRL: I'm hardly ever in class.

SYNCHRONIZED SWIMMER 1: And partly because she already knew that Shannon was sick.

SYNCHRONIZED SWIMMER 4: She'd been moved out of her house and into a hospital. But the Girl—

SHANNON: Never called.

SYNCHRONIZED SWIMMER 3: She never—

SHANNON: Sent a card.

SYNCHRONIZED SWIMMER 1: She never brought her a Whiz sandwich.

SYNCHRONIZED SWIMMER 5: And when it's announced over the PA that—

SHANNON: "Shannon Lishman passed away over the weekend."

DONNY: "Of bone cancer."

SYNCHRONIZED SWIMMER 2: "Fourteen years old."

BEN: "Top student."

SYNCHRONIZED SWIMMER 1: "Honour roll."

SYNCHRONIZED SWIMMER 4: The Girl feels nothing.

SYNCHRONIZED SWIMMER 3: She doesn't feel anything except a kind of fear that she's someone who doesn't feel.

SHANNON exits.

COACH CINDY: You're on my team. There's no escape. Well, that's not entirely true. There are a few options . . .

GIRL: Okay.

COACH CINDY: Oh, no, they won't work, you're too sensitive.

GIRL: I'll do anything!

COACH CINDY: Option one: arrange to meet him.

GIRL: Okay.

COACH CINDY: Somewhere dark.

GIRL: Uh huh?

COACH CINDY: Quiet.

GIRL: Yeah?

COACH CINDY: And when you're all alone, just the two of you . . .

GIRL: Yes?

COACH CINDY: Kill him.

GIRL: I-I'm sorry?

COACH CINDY: Oh, did I say kill him? I meant slit his throat. Oh dear, that's not what I meant either. Cut him loose.

GIRL: What's option two?

COACH CINDY: Go away. Go far, far away to a distant land. Somewhere near water. When night falls, and everyone is sleeping, swim out as far as you can go, until your legs lose strength and your arms collapse, until your eyes burn and your belly fills with water. Close your eyes, so that the moon no longer lights your way, and disappear into the seafoam.

GIRL: Like, kill myself?

COACH CINDY: It's worth a try! Either that, or . . .

GIRL: Yeah?

COACH CINDY: Go home and tell your mommy you've been fucking a drug-dealing pimp.

GIRL: No.

COACH CINDY: Well, I guess you're stuck then.

GIRL: I can't. I can't do that.

The GIRL's MOM enters in a bathing suit and shorts.

MOM: What can't you do, honey? You're late! Get your sun hat!

GIRL: My what?

DAD enters in a Guayabera shirt.

DAD: Your bathing suit. It's time for a family intervention. I mean, vacation.

COACH CINDY: Suck it up, sweetie! Put a smile on your face! And have fun in—!

SYNCHRONIZED SWIMMERS: CUBA! Cuba, Cuba!!

DAD: Guantanamera! Right, sweetheart?

COACH CINDY: HAHAHAHAHAHAHAHAHAHAHAHAHA!!!

Cuban music plays over COACH CINDY's laughter. The SYNCHRONIZED SWIMMERS animate into a full beach scene.

MOM: Flip-flops! Sunscreen! Snorkelling! Ping-Pong! Karaoke! Uh, what else?

DAD: Those bartenders are rather, uh . . . familiar.

MOM: They do like the girls.

DAD: But not in that way.

MOM: No! It's a good trip.

DAD: It's a great trip. Surf and sand! The wind sweeping in and rustling the palm leaves.

MOM: And they're safe! Right, honey?

DAD: Yeah, they're street smart. We've always given them the freedom to roam.

MOM: It's a learning experience!

DAD: A cultural experience. Let them run. Let them mix with the locals!

MOM: Drink virgin margaritas!

DAD: No alcohol.

MOM: Build giant castles in the sand!

DAD: Huge!

MOM: And I think—

DAD: You think?

MOM: Don't you?

DAD: We did the right thing.

MOM: In the nick of time.

DAD: In the nick of time.

MOM: We needed this.

DAD: As a family.

MOM: As a couple.

DAD: And our girls are safe.

GIRL: But what about Ty? He's probably in a basement somewhere. He's probably never been on a beach vacation and probably never will.

The SYNCHRONIZED SWIMMERS laugh.

His father was abusive.

WOMAN: *(rushing in)* He abused me!

There is more laughter from the SYNCHRONIZED SWIMMERS.

(grabbing the GIRL) You need to forget about him. You need to think about you!

SYNCHRONIZED SWIMMERS: Hey! Let go of her! Get out of here!

WOMAN: You get out! This isn't the Tryp Cayo Coco resort, people!

GIRL: It isn't?

WOMAN: No, it's the bathroom at the Rideau Centre! So cut the maracas and snap out of it!

The SYNCHRONIZED SWIMMERS retreat.

GIRL: If you don't like it, then leave.

WOMAN: I can't. If I try to sneak out, he'll see me.

GIRL: Who?

WOMAN: I'll just have to wait it out.

GIRL: Ty?

WOMAN: I'll stay in here forever if I have to.

GIRL: He's out there?

WOMAN: I'll call Paul, make something up—tell him I lost my wallet—

GIRL: In his spot?

WOMAN: I missed the bus, got into an accident—

GIRL: By the New York Fries?

WOMAN: I don't know, eating tater tots at the fucking TacoTime! I was stupid to meet him. There's no changing what happened. I've just made it worse.

GIRL: So you're just going to stay in here until the mall closes? Curl up into a ball and rot? Well, I'm not. I'm hungry. Where are the tater tots? I've never been so hungry in my life!

WOMAN: You're pregnant! In Cuba, you find out that you're pregnant.

Beat.

GIRL: Like, with a baby?

WOMAN: Like with a baby.

Beat.

GIRL: I'll move out. Support myself.

WOMAN: You're fourteen years old.

GIRL: Ty can get a job. We can get an apartment.

WOMAN: That won't happen.

GIRL: Does he know yet?

WOMAN: No.

GIRL: I need to tell him.

WOMAN: No, this has to stop. I'm putting an end to you.

Beat.

GIRL: How are you going to do that?

WOMAN: It's time for you to be gone from my life.

GIRL: Is that a threat? I'm not going to just evaporate into the air. And if I do, you do too.

WOMAN: Right.

GIRL: So, what are you going to do?

WOMAN: I don't know.

GIRL: Well, I guess I'm on my own then.

The GIRL exits. The WOMAN is left alone.

WOMAN: Yeah.

The WOMAN thinks for a long moment. There are haunting under-water sounds. A shadow passes overhead. The WOMAN remains on stage for the following two scenes.

Scene 10

TY enters wearing a flashy blazer.

TY: I like your tan.

GIRL: Thanks. I like your jacket.

TY moves in and they kiss.

TY: How was it?

GIRL: It was awesome! We stole beer out of the fridge when everyone was asleep and, and . . .

A knapsack is tossed on stage.

Oh yeah, I bought this knapsack with the sixty dollars my grandma gave me, but it was only, like, ten Cuban pesos, which is like ten American, which is like eight-fifty Canadian, so I still got, like, fifty-two left. See?

A bundle of US dollars are thrown on stage, which the GIRL catches.

That's American. Cool, huh?

The GIRL zips the money into her knapsack. TY clocks this.

TY: I did a lot of thinking when you were away.

GIRL: Me too.

TY: Yeah? What did you think about?

GIRL: You go first.

TY smiles.

TY: Okay. I wanna move outta my ma's. Get my own place and learn about business.

GIRL: You mean, like go to school?

TY: No, bigger than that. Start an enterprise from scratch. Something that will make us a lot of money. Now you. What did you think about?

GIRL: Same thing. Because, like, the thing is, I have to make a choice.

TY: What kinda choice?

GIRL: Like, between school and the team and you, because, obviously, Coach Cindy wants to own my fucking soul—

TY reaches in and picks something off the GIRL's face.

What?

TY looks at his fingers, then wipes them on his pants.

TY: Sparkles and shit.

GIRL: Why is that still there?

TY: What is it?

GIRL: Makeup from synchro.

TY: You gotta wash that shit off. You smell like a toilet bowl. Like bleach and shit.

GIRL: But . . . I haven't been to practice since before Cuba. *(wiping at her face)* That's fucking weird.

> *TY grabs her knapsack and puts it on his back.*

Hey!

TY: It fits! Let me showyousomeshit, show you some shit in this little Cuban knapsack. Come on!

GIRL: No! What? Ty!

> *Transition.*

TY: So there's Zach, right? See him up there?

GIRL: Uh huh.

TY: See what he's doing?

GIRL: He's standing there. Ty, I need to tell you something—

TY: He's scoping the whole fucking level. He's watching for—check this shit out. See that guy? He walks up, says hello to Zach, asks a question, Zach answers, and then, look, checkthatshitout. Who's that?

GIRL: Alisha!

(calls out) Hey, Alisha!

TY: Shut the fuck up!

He effortlessly slaps her.

Yer acting like a kid.

GIRL: Fuck you, don't do that.

She pushes him.

TY: He's fucking doing business, yo.

GIRL: I don't care, don't slap me.

TY: Calm down. People are looking.

He sighs, disappointed.

I'm trying to talk to you about something important.

GIRL: Okay, what were you going to say?

TY: Forget it.

GIRL: I'm sorry, Ty, just—

TY: I was going to tell you when it was special.

GIRL: What's Zach doing with that guy?

TY: He's talking business. Which is how I want to talk to you right now, but you ruined it.

GIRL: I'm sorry.

A Big Turk is tossed on stage. TY *catches it.*

TY: I got you something.

GIRL: A Big Turk?

TY: Yeah.

GIRL: Wow.

TY: No, no, it's just a joke. Here.

> *TY pulls a gold chain out of his jacket pocket.*

I want you to be my girl.

GIRL: I am your girl.

TY: No, but morethanthat.

GIRL: What do you mean, / like . . .

TY: Like what Alisha and Zach are doing: *representing* each other.

GIRL: Representing?

TY: Uh huh. I mean, he's got a few girls and bought a house and shit, but I just want to do it with you.

GIRL: Do what?

TY: Sell you. But like, respectfully. They'd love you.

> *A beat, as the GIRL takes in this new information.*

GIRL: Really?

TY: Why wouldn't they?

GIRL: Cuz I'm just like . . . I don't know. Skinny.

TY: They'd love you.

GIRL: Really?

TY: Yeah.

GIRL: Do you love me?

TY: Sure.

GIRL: Then why aren't you paying me?

TY: Cheekybitch. You do it for free, why not do it for money?

GIRL: I don't know. Cuz ... I'm not allowed to go out at night.

TY: You can sneak out.

GIRL: No.

TY: What do you mean, "no"? You do it all the time.

GIRL: I gotta go.

> *She grabs for the knapsack, but* TY *pulls it away, out of her reach.*

Gimme my knapsack, please.

TY: No, I need it for a down payment. I got a car.

GIRL: Ty, seriously.

TY: I'm serious. It's a four-door Mazda and shit.

GIRL: Ty! It's not funny!

TY: Okay, baby, come here. Come here, come here.

TY grabs her and the SYNCHRONIZED SWIMMERS rush on stage.

GIRL: What are you doing?

SYNCHRONIZED SWIMMER 3: Ty picks her up and pins her over a railing so that she is upside down, dangling over the food court atrium.

TY: You're my girl. You think you can just fuck off?

GIRL: Don't! I'm falling!

SYNCHRONIZED SWIMMER 2: She can hear the sound of water spurting up from the fountain below.

GIRL: Stop!!

SYNCHRONIZED SWIMMER 4: Her eyes are huge.

SYNCHRONIZED SWIMMER 1: People start looking.

GIRL: Fine! I'll give you the money!

TY pulls the GIRL up.

TY: Are you fucking crazy?

GIRL: Am I crazy? You almost killed me!

TY: You're such a fraud.

GIRL: I'm sorry.

SYNCHRONIZED SWIMMER 4: Ty takes the money out of the knapsack.

SYNCHRONIZED SWIMMER 5: And they head to the parking lot.

SYNCHRONIZED SWIMMER 3: And get into Ty's new—

SYNCHRONIZED SWIMMER 2: Used—

SYNCHRONIZED SWIMMER 1: Mazda.

GIRL: I don't want to have sex anymore.

TY: Why's that?

GIRL: I want to be pure.

TY laughs.

It's true.

TY: You calling the shots now?

SYNCHRONIZED SWIMMER 5: He pulls her pinky back.

GIRL: Ow, wait.

SYNCHRONIZED SWIMMER 3: It feels like he's going to break it.

GIRL: You're hurting me!

TY: Don't be such a drama queen.

GIRL: I don't want to have sex!

TY: So do something else then.

SYNCHRONIZED SWIMMER 2: He grabs her by the neck.

There is a sound of a baton beating against the side of the pool. One, two, three, four, five, six, seven, eight.

Transition.

Scene 11

MOM enters and delivers her lines to the WOMAN, who is still on stage. TY directs his lines to MOM.

MOM: The first time I saw Ty was a block from our house. I knew it was him because when I looked in his direction he turned away and hid his face.

TY: *(laughing)* Shit . . . what was I supposed to do? Go up and introduce myself?

MOM: At that time, I didn't know the full extent of things. I didn't want to jump to any conclusions. I did what I could. I'd call the dance club and plead with them, "She's only fourteen," and they'd say, "It's an underage club."

TY laughs.

So I'd drive down and wait outside. Sometimes she wasn't there. I never knew where to look. I was so angry. And worried. Worried and angry. Angry and worried. I kept hoping that the team would keep her on track. She was so good at it.

TY: She's good at a lot of things.

MOM: Then he started calling, and he wouldn't stop.

TY: You wouldn't answer.

MOM: She doesn't live here anymore!

TY: Where's she living, then? I'm not stupid.

MOM: She's at her grandma's.

TY: Her grandma doesn't live in Ottawa.

MOM: Her other grandma.

TY: Why's the light on in her bedroom, then?

MOM: I tried to get a restraining order, but the police told me that she would have to go to court, and I didn't want to put her through that.

TY: I was in jail then anyway.

MOM: I spoke to a police officer who was very understanding and assured me that he would let me know when he was released.

TY: A month later.

MOM: She was scared.

TY: What, like I'm the boogeyman? She knows exactly what she's doing.

MOM: What do you want? What do you want? What do you want? What do you want? What do you want?!

TY: I want you to lower your shrill-ass voice.

MOM: You have to understand. She's a sensitive girl. She's more worried about other people than herself. It's a good quality, until you meet someone who preys on that. It was a full year of worry. And then she stopped leaving bloodstains in her underwear. I didn't tell her dad. At first. I was afraid that he would judge her. That he wouldn't understand the situation. But it was just a matter of time before it all came out.

DAD storms onto the stage and the WOMAN exits.

DAD: He's not going to get away with this.

MOM: I'm sorry. I couldn't hide it.

DAD: *(to MOM)* You did hide it.

GIRL: It's not her fault.

The GIRL's SISTER enters.

SISTER: If this gets out, everyone will call you a slut.

GIRL: So? I like it!

SISTER: Okay, cool then—

The GIRL's BROTHER enters.

BROTHER: No, you don't.

GIRL: Yes, I do!

BROTHER: No, you don't.

MOM: Listen to your brother.

GIRL: Okay. I don't.

DAD: We'll press charges.

GIRL: No!! Dad, you can't—

BROTHER: You have to. You have to stand up for yourself!

GIRL: He's just some loser.

BROTHER: Have some dignity!

DAD: He had no right to fuck—!

(correcting) To *spend time* with my daughter.

MOM: Someone had to spend time with her.

DAD: What's that supposed to mean?

SISTER: You weren't around, Dad!

MOM: Stop shouting. It's not helping.

SISTER: Why aren't I allowed to shout? WHY IS EVERYONE ALLOWED TO SHOUT BUT ME?

BROTHER: *(to the GIRL)* This is your fault.

SISTER: *I've* fucked losers.

DAD & MOM: Language!

SISTER: Why don't I count as much as she does?

GIRL: You do!

MOM: She needed help!

BROTHER: She needed protection.

MOM: She was roaming the streets. She was—

DAD: *(whimpering)* My little girl, my little girl, my little girl . . .

GIRL: Dad, I'm still your little girl.

SISTER: You're *not* a little girl.

DAD: We're going to the police!

GIRL: NOOOO!!!

MOM: It will only make it worse.

DAD: He has to pay for this!

GIRL: It wasn't him. It was me. It was my fault.

DAD: We're going to press charges. He's a sex predator. He's a monster!

DAD exits.

GIRL: *(calling after her DAD)* NO! IF YOU GO TO THE POLICE, I WILL BURN THIS PLACE DOWN! I SWEAR I WILL!

MOM: Oh no, honey, don't do that—

GIRL: I WILL!

MOM: No, don't do that. I'll talk to Dad, I'll talk to Dad, I'll talk to Dad, I'll talk to Dad . . .

MOM exits.

BROTHER: How could you let this happen?

SISTER: *(to the BROTHER)* It's really not a big deal.

BROTHER: *(to the GIRL)* You're not going to get away with this.

The BROTHER *exits.*

SISTER: *(to the* BROTHER*)* You'll get over it.

GIRL: *(pleading)* Is there something wrong with me?

SISTER: You suck.

The SISTER *exits and the* GIRL *is left alone. The light flickers. A shadow passes over the surface above. An ominous sound compels the* GIRL *to lie down.*

GIRL: *(calling out to no one, scared)* You're right. I'm a fuck-up. I'm sorry. Where are you? I'm sorry! I want this to be over. I want it to end. Don't just leave me here. Where the fuck are you?!

Scene 12

Light streams through the windows. It is peaceful. The WOMAN *enters wearing a lab coat. She speaks with a Polish accent.*

GIRL: Who are you?

WOMAN: Dr. Morgentaler.

GIRL: Doctor?

WOMAN: You can call me Henry.

GIRL: I'm / scared.

WOMAN: Scared?

GIRL: Yeah. Who were those people outside?

WOMAN: The angry people?

GIRL: Yeah.

WOMAN: With the signs?

GIRL: Yeah. Why are they here?

WOMAN: They have strong ideas. About right and wrong.

GIRL: Oh.

Beat.

Are they right?

WOMAN: They think that they are, but I think that you have the right to make a choice. They say no choice. I say pro-choice.

GIRL: What if I feel like I don't have a choice?

WOMAN: Even more reason to make one. Without fear of being spat on. Did you choose to be here?

GIRL: Yes.

WOMAN: Do you want to be here?

GIRL: Not really. Honestly, I just want to eat a burger without throwing up.

WOMAN: Fair enough.

GIRL: Really? Well, that's not the whole thing. There's a lot of stuff going on, and it's like it's all happening at once, all these pieces I can't really put together. I don't *want* to be here. I feel bad about being here, like, I know it's wrong . . . I just wish that I was a grown-up. So that I could understand it better.

WOMAN: Don't sell yourself short. You might understand it now as well as you'll ever understand it.

GIRL: *(hopeful)* Really?

WOMAN: Being young is hard.

GIRL: Sometimes it feels like I'm drowning . . . What people think it is, and what it actually is . . . it's just like I'm, like I'm . . . / stuck between this world and another.

WOMAN: Stuck between this world another.

GIRL: Yeah . . .

> *Beat.*

(a little drugged-out on anaesthetic) You're very nice. I hope that I'm like you someday. How long will this take?

WOMAN: Not too long.

GIRL: Oh, good.

WOMAN: I'm just going to scrape the walls of your uterus. It'll pinch a little. But you'll feel much better when it's all done.

> *Over the following speech, the WOMAN removes her lab coat.*

COACH CINDY: The Girl feels her strongest in water. The deeper she goes, the more pressure there is. Like a hug. She wants to disappear. Down through the pipes and into the ocean. Seaweed knotting around her legs and arms, so that she will stay there—a girl forever.

WOMAN: I have never believed that anyone could actually love me.

GIRL: Because of me?

WOMAN: My body has never felt like mine to give.

GIRL: Because of me?

WOMAN: I don't feel worthy of anyone or anything and I look for any way to prove it. I've never had children. I spend hours of my life feeling like a failure and a fraud.

GIRL: And you're telling me this because . . .

WOMAN: I'm frightened to death of marriage. My boyfriend tries to love me, but I can't love him back, because—

GIRL: Of me. Because of me?

WOMAN: I smoke!

GIRL: Quit.

WOMAN: I'm contaminated.

GIRL: You want me to feel bad?

WOMAN: Sure.

GIRL: I feel bad.

　　　TY enters.

TY: I feel bad.

WOMAN: I should have pressed charges.

TY: It's too late for that now.

WOMAN: But I could still tell people. People you know.

TY: Who?

WOMAN: Your girlfriend?

TY: Which one?

WOMAN: Your kids. Your daughter and your son.

TY: What would you tell them? It was twenty-five years ago. I was a kid, too.

> *Beat.*

Yeah. You could tell my family and, yeah, that would probably wreck it for me.

> *Beat.*

What do you want?

> *The WOMAN turns to the GIRL.*

WOMAN: What do you want?

GIRL: I want to pinch his nose closed with nose plugs. I want to hold him under water until his lungs burn. Stuff his mouth full of the pages of a porn mag. Pick him up and throw him down an escalator.

WOMAN: But I don't.

TY: No?

WOMAN: No. Instead, I go home.

TY exits.

GIRL: Let me go with you.

Beat.

WOMAN: Paul's making dinner.

GIRL: It smells good.

WOMAN: "Where have you been?" he asks. I could lie, or I could tell him.

GIRL: Tell him what?

WOMAN: That I met a man today. I had a date in a food court with a man who hurt me, a long time ago, when I was a kid. How do I say that?

GIRL: Just say it.

WOMAN: I don't want to.

GIRL: I will.

Long beat.

WOMAN: What does he say?

GIRL: He doesn't say anything.

WOMAN: Right.

Beat.

GIRL: He moves in closer.

WOMAN: To you?

GIRL: To me.

WOMAN: Then what?

GIRL: I shake.

The GIRL exits. Over the following speech, the WOMAN cracks open, softens, just a bit.

WOMAN: He puts a hand on my chest and holds me against him and this calms me. And I think about how it feels to dance with him. I think about sleeping beside him—making coffee in the morning. I think about the sweat on his face when he's nervous or when it's a little hot outside. I think about the way that he looks at me when I get out of the shower. I think about him smiling and laughing at my jokes. I think about us. I think about looking him directly in the eye and feeling his breath on my cheek. About falling into one another. I think about love.

End.

Acknowledgements

Many thanks to the Canada Council for the Arts and the Ontario Arts Council Recommender Grants for Theatre Creators for supporting me throughout the writing of *Mortified*. To Nightwood Theatre for providing rehearsal space, and to Studio 180 for making *Mortified* part of its In Development program. Special thanks to my right and left hand in *Mortifed*'s first production: Dramaturge Jonathon Young and Director Anita Rochon. To Kathryn Shaw, David Hudgins, and Roy Surette for taking the leap and giving *Mortified* its first home. And to my ever-supportive and loving family: Eva, Bob, Lisa, Erik, and Karin.

Amy Rutherford is a Canadian playwright and actress who has worked for twenty years in TV, film, and theatre with some of the country's leading artists. A graduate of the National Theatre School of Canada and the Stratford Festival's Birmingham Conservatory, Amy has co-written several plays, including *The Public Servant* and *Out of the Woods*. She currently divides her time between Toronto and Vancouver with her partner Jonathon Young.

First edition: January 2022
Printed and bound in Canada by Imprimerie Gauvin, Gatineau

Jacket design by Monnet Design

PLAYWRIGHTS
CANADA PRESS

202-269 Richmond St. W.
Toronto, ON
M5V 1X1

416.703.0013
info@playwrightscanada.com
www.playwrightscanada.com
@playcanpress

MIX
Paper from
responsible sources
FSC   FSC® C100212
www.fsc.org